The True Tale of a GIANTESS

The Story of Anna Swan

Anne Renaud ✳ Marie Lafrance

Kids Can Press

TATAMAGOUCHE

When I was small, I was already big news.
From Pictou to Tatamagouche, people chattered about me.

PICTOU

They whispered over tea and gossiped across fences. They snooped around our farmhouse, buzzing about like flies. They craned their necks. They oohed and aahed. They stared with saucer eyes.

Would you like to know why?

Because when I was small, I was already

TREMENDOUS.

"All the more to love," cooed my parents.
By the time I was four years old, I had
sprouted higher than the Queen Anne's lace
that swayed in our meadow. Higher than
our sheep. Higher than our rain barrel.

My parents took me to county fairs to show me off.
Newspapers called me the Infant Giantess. My arms and
wrists were as long and large as those of a full-grown
man. I was a celebrity.

ANNA SWAN
THE INFANT GIANTESS

E CREAM

And still I grew.
Taller than my mother.
Taller than my father.

By the time I was twelve, I had risen higher than the hollyhocks that crowded our garden. Higher than our cows and horses. Higher than three bales of hay.

People chattered about me even more. Some followed me around making rude comments. They forgot I was not old enough to be so tall.

And still I grew.

On happy days, I did not have to squeeze into my world. Outside was my favorite place to be.

On glum days, I poked and bulged and jutted out from all sorts of spaces. No matter how small I folded myself, I simply did not fit.

And still I grew.

Being tall did have some advantages. My parents never, ever lost me in a crowd. I could reach the highest shelves. I always had the best view at parades and concerts.

By the time I was seventeen, I loomed higher than our sunflowers and cornstalks. Higher than everyone in Tatamagouche and the surrounding villages. Higher than the door of our general store.

I weighed as much as three goats, two turkeys, one duck and a rooster.

While I was growing in Nova Scotia, a man named Phineas Taylor Barnum was looking for people to join his Gallery of Wonders in his museum in New York City.

"The bigger the better. The smaller the better. The taller the better. The shorter the better," said Mr. Barnum.

My parents did not want me to leave, but I pestered them.

"I dream of a life of travel and adventure. No matter how scary, I need to find a way to fit."

"But you still have to go to school," they said.

"I can learn in New York City."

"But New York is too busy, too boisterous," they said.

"I dream of a life as big as me," I insisted.

And then it was!

I had many happy days in my new home at the museum.
I was fitted for fine dresses. Elegant shoes were fashioned
for my size 16½ feet. With my hair styled high on my head,
I stood eight feet tall. I performed in plays, recited poetry
and played piano for my spectators.

The people in the Gallery of Wonders became my friends. John Battersby was as skinny as a celery stick. Hannah, his wife, was as plump as a pillow. Minnie Warren and Commodore Nutt stood no higher than my knees. Noah Orr and Monsieur Joseph were like me and towered like totem poles.

I had glum days in New York City, too. When I missed my parents, brothers and sisters. When I was weary of people pointing and staring at me.

And I had very grim days. When, twice, fire devoured our museum. When smoke and flames took all we owned — and very nearly our lives!

But after each fire, Mr. Barnum opened a new museum, and we all moved back in.

Sometimes we boarded a ship and sailed beyond sunrises and sunsets, to faraway places.

I even had tea with the Queen of England!

It was on one of these trips that I fell in love.

He was known as the Kentucky Mountain Giant, but his real name was Martin Van Buren Bates. He, too, had to stoop and bend and fold himself into all sorts of spaces. Like me, he did not always fit.

We married in a church in London's Trafalgar Square. My friend the Queen asked her dressmakers to make my wedding gown. It billowed out around me like a cloud with dozens of yards of satin and lace.

After our wedding, Martin and I toured as
THE TALLEST MARRIED COUPLE ON EARTH.

Together we weighed almost half a ton.
As much as two burly brown bears. Windows
rattled, dishes clinked and floors groaned
wherever we walked.

Martin and I eventually tired of touring, so we decided to stay put. We chose the town of Seville, Ohio, because of its whispering streams and rolling fields. It reminded me of my Nova Scotia home.

We built a house that was tall at the front for Martin and me, and short at the back for friends and family. We also built a barn for our farm animals and my pet monkey, Buttons.

At last, we had a life where everyone fit.

Author's Note

The giantess Anna Swan really did exist. She was born on August 6, 1846, near Tatamagouche, in the farming community of Millbrook, Nova Scotia. At birth, she weighed 6 kg (13 lb.), almost twice the weight of an average newborn.

By four years old, Anna weighed over 45 kg (100 lb.) and measured 1.4 m (4 ft., 8 in.). By the time she was six years old, she measured 1.7 m (5 ft., 6 in.), surpassing her mother by 5 cm (2 in.) and standing eye to eye with her father. At twelve years old, Anna measured well over 1.8 m (6 ft.), and when she stopped growing at age seventeen, she stood 2.4 m (7 ft., 11.5 in.) tall and weighed over 181 kg (400 lb.).

Anna attracted the interest of showman Phineas Taylor Barnum, who invited her to New York City. Anna's parents agreed to let her go on the condition that she be provided with a private tutor for three years so she could continue her studies in music and literature. This tutor was to act as her chaperone, as it was not proper for a young lady to be without one at the time. As well, Anna's mother was to remain with her in New York until she turned eighteen.

Anna was billed as the Tallest Girl in the World at Barnum's American Museum, a combination zoo, art gallery, aquarium, concert hall and museum. She later traveled throughout North America and Europe. In England, she was received by Queen Victoria. In 1871, Anna married Martin Van Buren Bates, also known as the Kentucky Mountain Giant. Martin was slightly shorter than Anna, standing 2.3 m (7 ft., 8 in.) tall. The couple had two children: a girl in 1872 and a boy in 1879. Sadly, neither of them survived. Anna and Martin settled in Seville, Ohio, in the mid-1870s, where they built a house big enough for both of them and bred horses and cattle. Over the years, Anna's health had been failing, and on August 5, 1888, she died unexpectedly from heart failure. It was the eve of her forty-second birthday.

It is not entirely clear what caused Anna's spectacular growth. It may have been a rare medical condition called pituitary gigantism. This is caused by an excess of growth hormone due to a pituitary adenoma, a type of brain tumor.

Anna at age 17 with her parents

Promotional card of Anna with people of average height

Phineas Taylor Barnum

The tumor affects the pituitary gland, which influences growth.

Today, Anna's legacy is lovingly preserved both in Ohio and Nova Scotia. Visitors to Seville are met with a road sign commemorating Anna's and Martin's lives. Artifacts, including replicas of their clothing, are showcased at the Seville Historical Museum.

In Nova Scotia, a monument was erected near Tatamagouche in honor of Anna, recounting the highlights of her extraordinary life. There is also the Creamery Square Heritage Centre, where visitors can view artifacts of Anna's life and learn more about the loving, kind-hearted giantess who touched the lives of many with her grace, dignity and compassion.

*Martin Van Buren Bates, Anna Swan and
an unknown person*

Author's Sources

BOOKS

Blakeley, Phyllis R. *Nova Scotia's Two Remarkable Giants.* Hantsport, NS: Lancelot Press, 1970.

Giles Millard, Ellen. *Big Annie: The Nova Scotia Giantess.* The Colchester Printing Company, 2008.

Holt Gramly, Allene. *The World's Tallest Couple.* Mansfield, OH: Appleseed Press, 1983.

Langille, Jacqueline. *Giants Angus McAskill and Anna Swan.* Tantallon, NS: Four East Publications Ltd., 1990.

Renaud, Anne. *The Extraordinary Life of Anna Swan.* Cape Breton University Press, 2013.

Vacon, Shirley Irene. *Giants of Nova Scotia: The Lives of Anna Swan and Angus McAskill.* East Lawrencetown, NS: Pottersfield Press, 2008.

MAGAZINE ARTICLES

Burden, George. "The Giantess of Nova Scotia." *The Medical Post*, March 3, 1998.

Burrows, Mary. "Anna Swan: Nova Scotia's Famed Giantess." *Chatelaine*, December 1966.

NEWSPAPERS

The Nova Scotian, July 14, 1851.

New York Daily Tribune, November 17, 1863.

The New York Times, January 26, 1864.

The New York Times, February 2, 1869.

Illustrated Times, March 20, 1869.

Illustrated London News, June 24, 1871.

The Seville Times, August 5, 1888.

To those of us who sometimes feel we do not fit — A.R.

For all my friends who think they don't fit, the story of a brave young lady who finally did — M.L.

My deepest gratitude to both Dale Swan and Diane Shink, great-grandnephew and great-grandniece of Anna Swan, as well as Rhonda Cookenour, third great-grandniece of Martin Van Buren Bates, who generously shared their precious family history, photographs and artifacts. And to Adrienne Saint-Pierre, curator of the Barnum Museum in Bridgeport, Connecticut, for her knowledge of all things Barnum. Last, but far from least, to my editor, Jennifer Stokes, for elevating my work.

The author acknowledges the support of the Canada Council for the Arts.

PHOTO CREDITS

Every reasonable effort has been made to trace ownership of, and give accurate credit to, copyrighted material. Information that would enable the publisher to correct any discrepancies in future editions would be appreciated.

p. 30: Photo of Anna and her parents courtesy of the Nova Scotia Museum.
p. 30: Photo of Phineas Taylor Barnum courtesy of the Library of Congress.
p. 30: Promotional card of Anna with people of average height courtesy of Diane Gudatis.
p. 31: Photo of Martin Van Buren Bates, Anna Swan and an unknown person courtesy of Matt Swain.

Kids Can Press gratefully acknowledges the financial support of the Government of Ontario, through the Ontario Media Development Corporation; the Ontario Arts Council; the Canada Council for the Arts; and the Government of Canada, through the CBF, for our publishing activity.

Published in Canada and the U.S. by Kids Can Press Ltd.
25 Dockside Drive, Toronto, ON M5A 0B5

Kids Can Press is a Corus Entertainment Inc. company

www.kidscanpress.com

The artwork in this book was rendered in mixed media and Photoshop. The text is set in Catalina Clemente.

Edited by Jennifer Stokes
Designed by Marie Bartholomew

Printed and bound in Malaysia, in 3/2018 by Tien Wah Press (Pte.) Ltd.
CM 18 0 9 8 7 6 5 4 3 2 1

LIBRARY AND ARCHIVES CANADA CATALOGUING IN PUBLICATION

Renaud, Anne, 1957–, author
    The true tale of a giantess: the story of Anna Swan / written by Anne Renaud ; illustrated by Marie Lafrance.

Includes bibliographical references.
ISBN 978-1-77138-376-9 (hardcover)

1. Swan, Anna, 1846–1888 – Juvenile literature. 2. Giants – Nova Scotia – Biography – Juvenile literature. I. Lafrance, Marie, illustrator II. Title.

GN69.22.S9R453 2018   j599.9'49   C2017-906646-3